EDGE BOOKS

DRAWING COOL STUFF

HOW TO DRAW

FEROCIOUS DINOSAURS

by Aaron Sautter

illustrated by Cynthia Martin

Capstone
press

Mankato, Minnesota

Edge Books are published by Capstone Press,
151 Good Counsel Drive, P.O. Box 669, Mankato, Minnesota 56002.
www.capstonepress.com

Library of Congress Cataloging-in-Publication Data
Sautter, Aaron.
    How to draw ferocious dinosaurs / by Aaron Sautter; illustrated by Cynthia Martin.
    p. cm.—(Edge books. Drawing cool stuff)
    Includes bibliographical references and index.
    Summary: "Lively text and fun illustrations describe how to draw ferocious
dinosaurs"—Provided by publisher.
    ISBN–13: 978-1-4296-0076-7 (hardcover)
    ISBN–10: 1-4296-0076-4 (hardcover)
    1. Dinosaurs in art—Juvenile literature. 2. Drawing—Technique—Juvenile
literature. I. Martin, Cynthia, 1961– II. Title. III. Series.
NC780.5.S28 2008
743'.85679—dc22   2007003452

Credits
Jason Knudson, designer

1 2 3 4 5 6 12 11 10 09 08 07

TABLE OF CONTENTS

WELCOME!

You probably chose this book because you think dinosaurs are awesome and cool. Or you picked it because you like to draw. Whatever the reason, get ready to dive into the world of ferocious dinosaurs!

Dinosaurs roamed the earth millions of years ago. Some were wily hunters. Others were gentle plant-eaters with wicked defenses. Whether you like Velociraptors or the mighty Tyrannosaurus rex, one thing is certain—you definitely wouldn't want to meet one in person!

This book is just a starting point. Once you've learned how to draw the awesome dinosaurs in this book, you can start drawing your own. Let your imagination run wild, and see if you can create a whole new ferocious dinosaur!

To get started, you'll need some supplies:

1. First you'll need drawing paper. Any type of blank, unlined paper will do.

2. Pencils are the easiest to use for your drawing projects. Make sure you have plenty of them.

3. You have to keep your pencils sharp to make clean lines. Keep a pencil sharpener close by. You'll use it a lot.

4. As you practice drawing, you'll need a good eraser. Pencil erasers wear out very fast. Get a rubber or kneaded eraser. You'll be glad you did.

5. When your drawing is finished, you can trace over it with a black ink pen or thin felt-tip marker. The dark lines will really make your work stand out.

6. If you decide to color your drawings, colored pencils and markers usually work best. You can also use colored pencils to shade your drawings and make them more lifelike.

APATOSAURUS

Imagine you're on a trip backward through time. Millions of years ago, the Apatosaurus roamed the land looking for plants to eat. This gentle giant used its long, curved neck to reach the highest leaves on the tallest trees.

STEP 1

After you've practiced this dinosaur, make him reach for some leaves high up at the top of a tree!

STEP 2

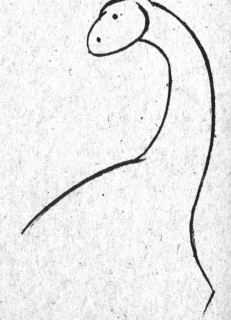

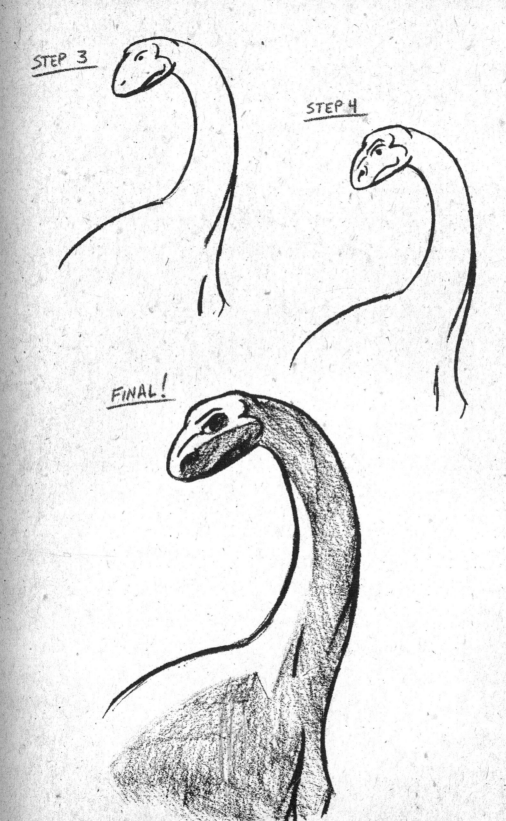

STEP 3

STEP 4

FINAL!

7

LUNCH TIME!

If you're lucky, you might get to see a young Apatosaurus and its mother eating some fresh green plants for lunch. Don't get too close, though. If Mom thinks you're a threat, she may try to squash you with her huge feet!

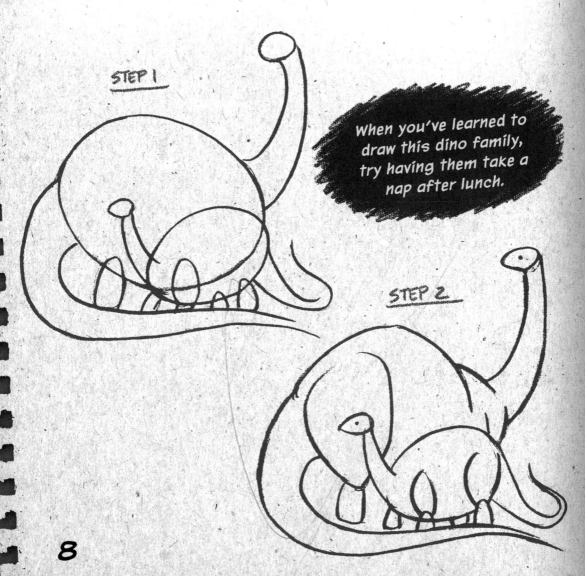

STEP 1

When you've learned to draw this dino family, try having them take a nap after lunch.

STEP 2

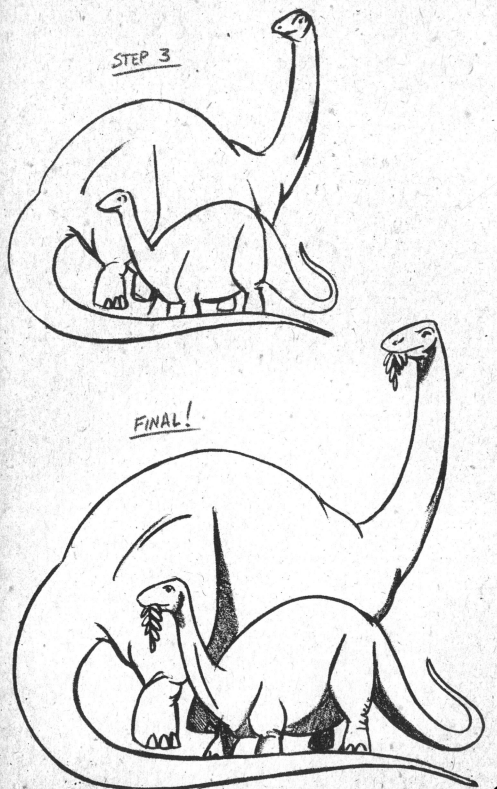

STEP 3

FINAL!

9

PLESIOSAUR

Thinking about going for a swim? You wouldn't want to if a Plesiosaur was in the water. These huge ocean-dwelling reptiles could grow bigger than a school bus! Plesiosaurs used their long necks and dagger-like teeth to snap up fish in a flash.

After drawing this dinosaur, try making your own fearsome ocean hunter.

STEP 1

STEP 2

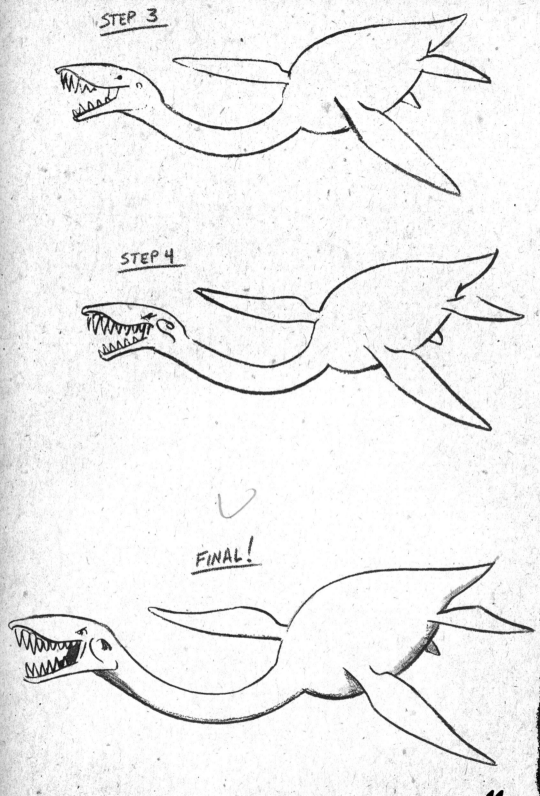

STEP 3

STEP 4

FINAL!

PTERANODON

Keep an eye on the sky for the Pteranodon! These flying reptiles had wings that stretched about 30 feet wide. If you saw a Pteranodon's shadow fly overhead, you'd want to find a safe shelter in a hurry!

After drawing this reptile, try giving it a tasty snack to carry in its claws.

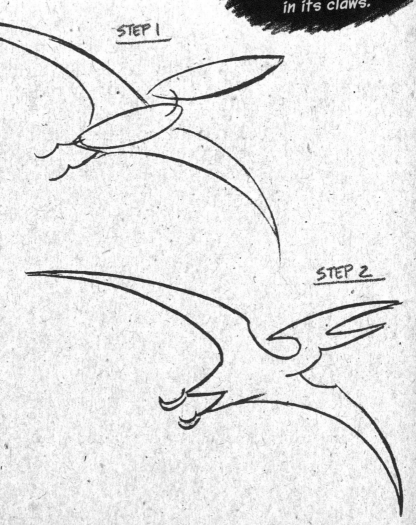

STEP I

STEP 2

STEP 3

STEP 4

FINAL!

13

TYRANNOSAURUS REX

Here's a face you don't want to see up close. The Tyrannosaurus rex was a meat-eating machine. Its razor-sharp teeth made quick meals out of smaller creatures. Don't let him find you, or you might be next on the menu!

STEP 1

After you've practiced this dinosaur, try adding some drool or a scar to make him really terrifying!

STEP 2

STEP 3

STEP 4

FINAL!

T-Rex Action!

The T-rex was a vicious hunter. It attacked other dinosaurs by ripping into them with its powerful jaws and huge back claws. Most creatures kept a sharp eye out for this fearsome predator.

STEP 1

After you've mastered the T-rex, try out the dinosaur fight on page 26!

STEP 2

STEP 3

STEP 4

FINAL!

SPINOSAURUS

Even the mighty T-rex would have a hard fight against the gigantic Spinosaurus. This huge dinosaur was one of the biggest meat-eaters of all time. Even the spines on its back stood more than 6 feet tall. You definitely don't want this monster coming after you!

After you've practiced this vicious dinosaur, try putting him in a fight with a T-rex and see who wins!

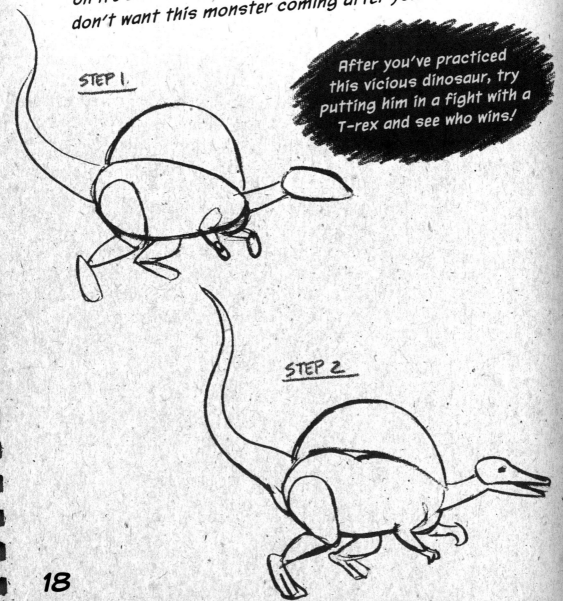

STEP 1.

STEP 2.

STEP 3

STEP 4

FINAL!

19

STEGOSAURUS

Watch out for that tail! Stegosaurus had a wicked defense against predators. Long, sharp spikes on the end of its tail kept enemies at a distance. Large back plates also kept hungry predators from chomping down on this dinosaur.

After drawing this dinosaur, try giving him some nasty battle scars from a fight!

STEP 1

STEP 2

STEP 3

STEP 4

FINAL!

21

TRICERATOPS

If the Triceratops charges, you'd better get out of the way fast! This dinosaur really lived up to its name, which means "three-horned face." It used its three large horns as an effective defense against predators.

STEP 1

Once you've practiced drawing this dinosaur, be sure to try out the dino fight on page 26!

STEP 2

STEP 3

STEP 4

FINAL!

23

VELOCIRAPTOR

This creature looks strange, but don't be fooled. The Velociraptor was a fast and deadly hunter. It could run up to 40 miles per hour. Its wicked claws and needlelike teeth easily tore into its prey.

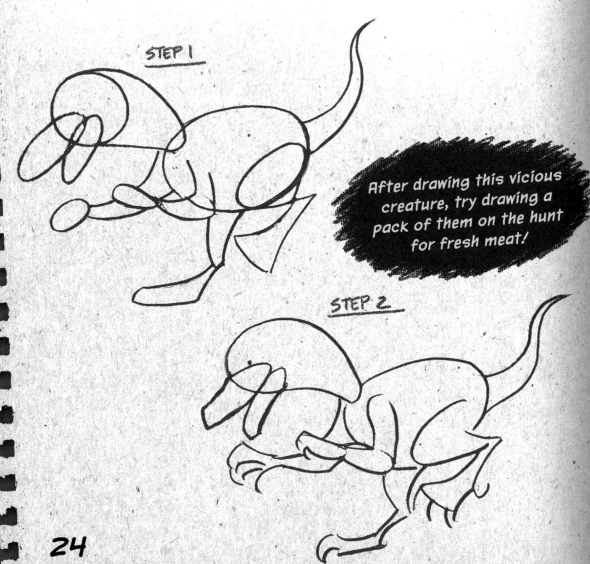

STEP 1

After drawing this vicious creature, try drawing a pack of them on the hunt for fresh meat!

STEP 2

STEP 3

STEP 4

FINAL!

25

DINO FIGHT!

Don't get in the middle of this fight! One wrong move and the T-rex might decide that you'd be an easier meal. Or you might have to run from the Triceratops and his three huge horns. Which dino do you think will win?

Once you've mastered this dino fight, try it again with the other dinosaurs from this book.

STEP 1

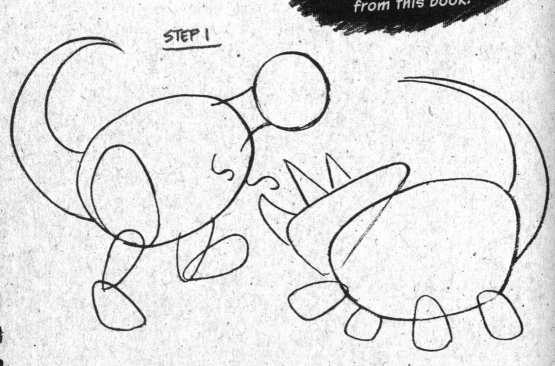

STEP 2

STEP 3

TO FINISH THIS DRAWING,
TURN TO THE NEXT PAGE!

27

STEP 4

STEP 5

28

STEP 6

FINAL!

GLOSSARY

defense (di-FENSS)—an ability to protect oneself from harm

ferocious (fuh-ROH-shuhss)—fierce and savage

gigantic (jye-GAN-tik)—huge or enormous

menu (MEN-yoo)—a list of food and drink choices

predator (PRED-uh-tur)—an animal that hunts and eats other animals for food

prey (PRAY)—an animal hunted and eaten by another animal for food

threat (THRET)—a creature or condition that can be considered to be dangerous

vicious (VISH-uhss)—fierce or dangerous

wily (WHY-lee)—smart and crafty

READ MORE

LaPlaca, Michael. *Dinosaurs and Other Prehistoric Animals.* How to Draw. New York: Scholastic, 2004.

Miller, Steve. *Thunder Lizards: How to Draw Fantastic Dinosaurs.* New York: Watson-Guptill, 2005.

Muehlenhardt, Amy Bailey. *Drawing and Learning About Dinosaurs: Using Shapes and Lines.* Sketch It! Minneapolis: Picture Window Books, 2004.

INTERNET SITES

FactHound offers a safe, fun way to find Internet sites related to this book. All of the sites on FactHound have been researched by our staff.

Here's how:
1. Visit *www.facthound.com*
2. Choose your grade level.
3. Type in this book ID code **1429600764** for age-appropriate sites. You may also browse subjects by clicking on letters, or by clicking on pictures and words.
4. Click on the **Fetch It** button.

FactHound will fetch the best sites for you!

Index